Handmade
Glass Painting
Greetings

A big thank you to my inspirational
friend Martin Duce

Handmade
Glass Painted
Greetings Cards

Judy Balchin

SEARCH PRESS

First published in Great Britain 2002

Search Press Limited
Wellwood, North Farm Road,
Tunbridge Wells, Kent TN2 3DR

Reprinted 2003, 2004

Text copyright © Judy Balchin
Photographs by Lotti de la Bédoyère, Search Press Studios
Photographs and design copyright © Search Press Ltd. 2002

ISBN 0 85532 988 2

If you have difficulty obtaining any of the equipment or materials mentioned in this book, please visit our website at **www.searchpress.com.**

Alternatively, you can write to the Publishers, at the address above, for a current list of stockists, including firms which operate a mail-order service.

> **Publishers' note**
> All the step-by-step photographs in this book feature the author, Judy Balchin, demonstrating how to make handmade greetings cards. No models have been used.

Printed in Spain by A. G. Elkar S. Coop. 48180 Loiu (Bizkaia)

I would like to thank John Wright of Pebeo UK Ltd. for supplying the paints used in this book. Special thanks go to the friendly team at Search Press, who have been so helpful and enthusiastic during its writing. In particular, Editorial Director Roz Dace for her guidance; editor Ally Howard for all her hard work and support; Juan Hayward for his creative design skills and Lotti de la Bédoyère for her photography. Finally, a big thank you to all the glass painting enthusiasts I have met over the years.

Cover
Sparkle tree *Coloured gems add sparkle to this alternative seasonal greetings card.*

Page 1
Hearts 'n' squares *This contemporary card is very easy to paint but looks stunning.*

Page 3
Glitter Daisy *Floral designs can be enhanced with a glittery border.*

Page 5
Jewelled flowers *The centres of the flowers on this card are embellished with jewels.*

Contents

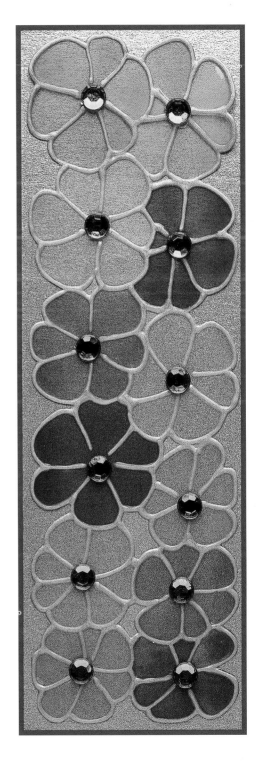

Introduction

Handmade greetings cards and gift tags are always fun to make and a delight to receive. Many of my relatives and friends have actually framed cards that I have made, which is a compliment to me as well as a continuing pleasure for them.

The title of this book may seem a little worrying, so let me explain: no glass is actually used for the cards featured. The book shows how glass painting techniques can be used on clear acetate, which is then mounted on, or framed by, card. Whether you are a beginner, or an old hand looking for new ideas, you should find something to interest you. Anyone new to glass painting will find it an inexpensive way to sample the delights of this fascinating hobby.

The projects are planned to take you on a slow and enjoyable learning curve, introducing new techniques as you progress. Techniques covered include outlining and painting; diluting the glass paints to achieve more subtle pastel effects; the production of 'mosaics', and the creation of shaped and window cards. From simple but stylish to outrageously glitzy, you should find inspiration in these pages.

Most of the designs are relatively simple. The bold outlines filled with vibrant, transparent colour can stand alone or can be enhanced for that extra sparkle. The designs and techniques can be adapted to create fridge magnets, mobiles or bookmarks, or worked on glass to make pictures, decorate plates and vases, and much more.

Part of the fun of creating your own masterpiece is browsing through the wonderful array of backing cards and papers available, and choosing coloured gems, glitter or other items for decoration. You can keep your cards simple, or make them as ornate as your imagination allows. My main problem is knowing just when to stop!

As you work through the book, your glass painting skills will develop. Try combining elements, taking a border from here, a motif from there, to create a new design. Do not discard ideas as you experiment with the outliners and paints: what can at first seem a mistake may spark off something new and exciting. I hope that by sharing my techniques and flights of fancy, I have provided a launch pad for your own ideas. Glass painting is both therapeutic and addictive. I should know: I have been doing it for ten years and am still enjoying every minute. My best advice is to enjoy your hobby. Have fun!

Judy.

Opposite: a selection of handmade cards. All the patterns can be found in this book.

Materials

1 Outliners Designs are usually outlined before painting. Black, silver, gold and white outliners are used in this book. Outliners for glass painting are squeezed from a tube to produce a raised line which, when dry, will contain the paint. It may be helpful to practise on an off-cut of acetate until you are able to achieve an even, unbroken line with the outliner.

2 Technical Pen A technical pen with a 0.5mm nib is used to produce a fine outline for more detailed work. The line it produces is flat. Solvent-based paints should be used to fill in the design.

3 Draughting Film Ink Use this water-based ink in the technical pen. It is designed to adhere to smooth surfaces.

4 White Spirit Use this to clean brushes which have been used with solvent-based paints.

5 Palette Use this to mix the paints. To create pastel shades, dilute the paints in a palette with clear glass paint.

6 Water Use this to clean water-based paint from brushes.

7 Paintbrushes Use round synthetic brushes to apply glass paint. A No.4 brush is ideal for most projects, though a smaller size may be used for small areas. A flat wash brush is used to cover large areas with glass paint (see the 'mosaic' project on page 25).

Glass paints These transparent paints developed for glass are also ideal for painting on acetate. They can be water- or solvent-based and different types should not be mixed. The paint should be applied generously to the outlined section and left to settle flat for a smooth effect. To avoid creating air bubbles, do not shake the bottle before use, and when mixing paints in your palette, do so gently.

Solvent-based paints These paints are generally more durable than water-based paints, but they take longer to dry. They can be diluted with clear paint from the same range to create pastel tones. Make sure you work in a well-ventilated room. Brushes should be cleaned with white spirit.

Water-based paints These paints dry quickly and have very little odour. Do not use water to dilute them as this will affect the viscosity – use clear paint from the same range. Brushes used with water-based paints can be cleaned with water.

White paint The only opaque glass paint is white (see page 31). The paint should be stirred gently in the bottle before applying to the acetate. A range of opaque pastels can be produced by adding coloured glass paint to white glass paint.

Methylated spirit Use this to clean the acrylic sheet thoroughly to ensure there are no smears (*not shown*).

• Hold the outliner tube firmly between your thumb and forefinger and squeeze it gently.

Using outliner

• Wipe the nozzle frequently with absorbent paper to keep it clean.

• To produce straight lines, try the 'touch, lift and pull' technique: touch the acetate gently with the tip, squeeze the tube, then lift the tip off the surface and pull it along, a bit like icing a cake!

• If the tube starts to 'ooze', squeeze it gently on either side of the top to stop the flow.

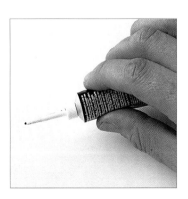

Other Materials

You will not need all the items on this page to start your glass painting. Each project provides you with a specific list which should be checked before you begin.

1 Hole punch Useful to make holes for ribbon in gift tags.

2 Masking tape Used to secure the acetate sheet to a base card or over a design.

3 Eraser Used to remove pencil lines when creating a window or shaped card.

4 Thick card Secure the acetate and design to this to prevent warping when outlining and painting.

5 Tracing paper Used to transfer a design to card to make a template (see page 43).

6 Rule Use with scissors to score a fold in a card or to measure and draw straight lines.

7 Cutting mat Use this when cutting card with a scalpel.

8 Double sided tape This is used in the birthday card project (see page 38) to secure the acetate design within the window card.

9 Double sided adhesive pads Use these to secure the painted designs to a base card to give a three-dimensional affect.

10 Pencil Use a pencil to trace your design or to draw it on to card.

11 Scissors Small, sharp pointed scissors are used to cut round acetate and card. They can be used to score card to create a fold.

12 Water-based felt tip pen Use this to draw round a template laid over painted acetate (see page 43).

13 Scalpel Use this with a cutting mat to trim card or acetate to size.

14 Cotton buds Used to wipe away outliner mistakes or small painting errors.

15 Strong clear adhesive Used to secure larger gems to finished painted designs.

Opposite:

Lighter fuel Use this or methylated spirit to wipe over the surface of the acetate to remove any traces of grease.

Spray adhesive Use to secure the painted design to the backing card.

PVA adhesive Use to secure decorative items such as plastic eyes or gems to your design.

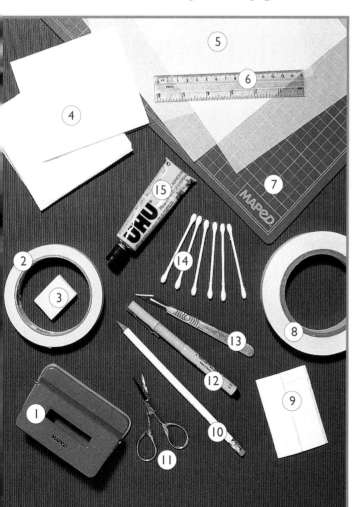

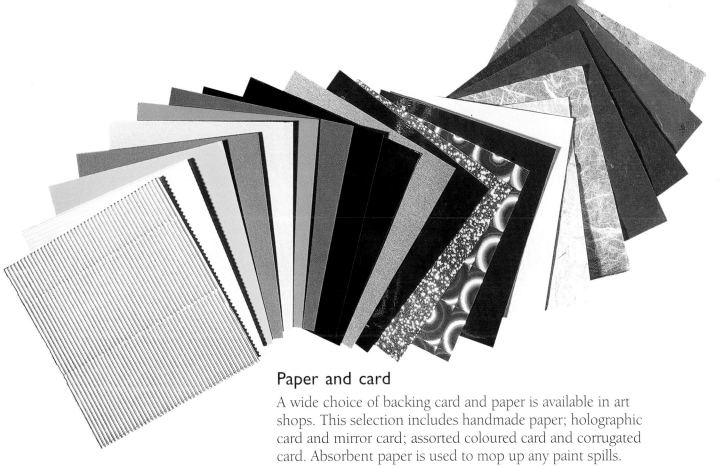

Paper and card

A wide choice of backing card and paper is available in art shops. This selection includes handmade paper; holographic card and mirror card; assorted coloured card and corrugated card. Absorbent paper is used to mop up any paint spills.

Finishing touches

Glitter, ribbon, brightly-coloured 'gems', feathers, plastic 'wobbly' eyes – all these can be used to enhance your cards ... let your imagination run riot!

Spray adhesive, PVA adhesive and lighter fluid

Crazy cat

Simplicity is the key to this first project. Achieving a good, even outline may take practice, but if you persevere the results will be well worth the effort. Vibrant colours and the addition of wobbly eyes gives this cat a humorous, quirky appearance which will definitely bring a smile to the face of the recipient. Animals are a fun subject, and as your confidence increases you might even decide to base a card on a favourite pet.

To begin with, you may find it helpful to photocopy the design from the book. Cut it to size and tape it to a piece of thick card. Acetate sheet tends to warp slightly when the outliner and paints are applied, so tape it down over the design before you start to make sure your working surface is completely flat.

You will need

Thick white card

Yellow card 8 x 9.5cm
(3¼ x 3¾ in)

Green card 18 x 10.5cm
(7 x 4⅛ in)

Acetate sheet 9 x 10cm
(3½ x 4⅛ in)

Black outliner

Glass paint: red and yellow

Brush No. 4

Plastic 'wobbly' eyes x 2

Small, pointed scissors

Masking tape

Spray adhesive

Rule or straight edge

Newspaper

Full-size template

Before you begin

To make sure the acetate is clean and grease-free, wipe it all over using absorbent paper which has been dampened with methylated spirit or lighter fuel.

1. Place the design on thick card. Cover it with the piece of acetate and tape it flat using masking tape.

2. Carefully squeeze on two blobs of outliner where the eyes will be positioned.

3. While the outliner is still wet, place a small plastic 'wobbly' eye on each blob and press it gently into place. Picking up the eye will be easier if you moisten your fingertip first.

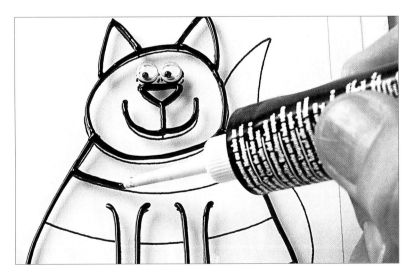

4. Beginning at the top and working downwards to prevent smudging, outline the cat carefully. Leave your work to dry.

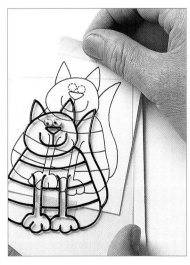

5. Lift the masking tape and carefully remove the template.

6. Paint in the yellow head, taking care to paint around the eyes, then the yellow stripes, legs and paws.

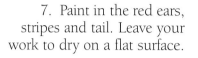

7. Paint in the red ears, stripes and tail. Leave your work to dry on a flat surface.

8. Cut round the edge of the cat with small sharp scissors.

9. Lay the cat face down on a piece of newspaper and cover with spray adhesive.

10. Press the cat into the centre of the rectangle of yellow card.

11. Use a cutting board, rule and the points of scissors to score down the centre of the rectangle of green card.

12. Coat the back of the yellow card with spray adhesive and press firmly to the front of the green card.

The finished card
*The head of the cat has been used for
the matching gift tag.*

Templates

gift tags

Templates on this page are shown full size.

Mother's Day

What mother would not be absolutely delighted to receive a beautifully-painted basket of flowers on her special day? This project shows how to make a cut-out card, which makes the flowers look even more convincing.

Sometimes, especially when there is no light shining through the acetate, glass paints can look a little dense. This project uses glass paints which have been diluted to produce a more pastel effect. The paints should be diluted with a clear, glass painting medium or with varnish. Do not use water or white spirit, and if in doubt ask your local craft shop.

You will need

White card 13 x 16cm
(5⅛ x 6¼ in)

Acetate sheet slightly smaller
than the card

Glass paints: pink, purple,
green and clear

Palette

Scissors

Masking tape

Paintbrush No.4

Pencil

Scalpel

Cutting mat

Spray adhesive

Full-size template

gift tag template

1. Fix the design to thick white card using masking tape. Secure the acetate over the design and outline it carefully. Leave it to dry.

2. Pour a little clear glass paint into a palette and add a few drops of pink glass paint. With your paintbrush, mix the paints together gently to avoid creating air bubbles.

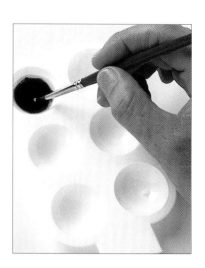

3. Use the diluted pink glass paint to paint half the tulips.

4. Make a mix of diluted purple glass paint and use it to paint the rest of the tulips. With a diluted green glass paint mix, complete the leaves and stems.

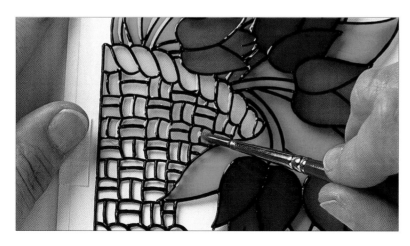

5. Paint the basket with diluted yellow glass paint, applying it more thickly in some areas for a more intense effect. Leave to dry.

6. Cut round the design using small scissors.

7. Score the white card down the middle, and fold. Cover the reverse of the design with spray adhesive and place on the front of the card, butting it up to the fold.

8. Open the card and place it on a cutting mat. Use a scalpel to trim off any excess card from around the outlines of the flowers.

9. Close the card and use a pencil to draw the outline of the flowers and leaves on to the inside back panel of the card.

10. Following the pencil lines, use a scalpel to cut off any excess card from around the outlines of the flowers.

The finished card and gift tag

Templates

Note

The card templates on this page have been reduced in size. To use, photocopy with the setting at 162 per cent.

gift tags - full- size

22

Sea Horse

The wonderfully translucent quality of glass paint lends itself perfectly to this card with a sea theme. Painted acetate is cut into mosaic squares to create an unusual border for the sea horse. The use of silver outliner means you have to be more accurate, as paint which overlaps the outliner will discolour it. This can be overcome to some extent by making a very weak solution of the turquoise paint to produce a 'watery' effect. Backing the completed sea horse with reflective mirror card adds an extra glow. The gift tag is made from a scrap of card decorated with mosaic 'tiles'.

You will need

Thick white card 10 x 22cm
(4 x 8¾ in)

Thick white card 8 x 13cm
(3¼ x 5¼ in)

Acetate sheet 6 x 15cm
(2³⁄₈ x 5⁷⁄₈ in)

Acetate sheet off-cut for mosaic

Mirror card: small piece

Outliners: silver & black

Glass paint: turquoise
and clear

Palette

Flat wash brush 1.25cm
(½ in)

Watercolour paper 18 x 21cm
(7 x 8¼ in)

Small scissors

Rule or straight edge

PVA adhesive

Double-sided adhesive pads

Masking tape

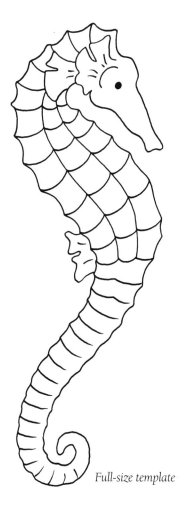

Full-size template

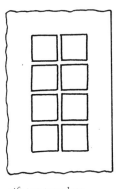

gift tag template

24

1. Tape the acetate off-cut on to thick white card to stop it warping as the paint dries.

2. Pour clear glass paint in a palette and add a few drops of turquoise glass paint. Paint the acetate with long, even strokes using a large wash brush, then leave it to dry.

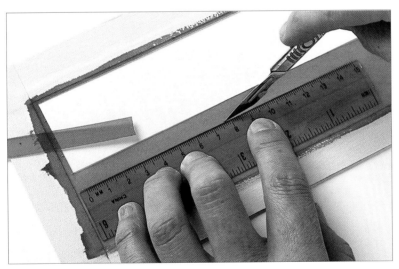

Note

If you are too impatient to wait, you can move on to complete steps 7-8 while you wait for the acetate to dry.

3. Using a scalpel and rule, cut the painted acetate strip into 1cm (³/₈ in) strips. This can be done without taking the acetate out of the frame.

4. Using scissors, cut the strips into 1cm (³/₈ in) squares to form the 'tiles'.

5. Score the watercolour paper and fold it in half. Carefully tear a 1cm (³/₈ in) strip from each edge.

6. Glue a border of squares round the edge of the paper, adding an extra row at the top and bottom for balance.

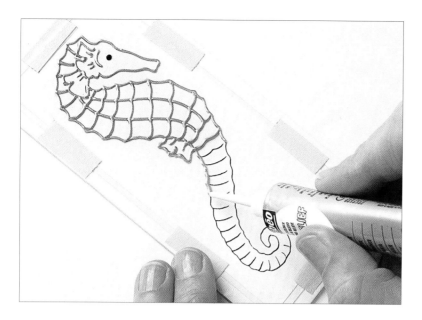

7. Place the sea horse template between the thick card and the small piece of acetate and tape it down. Dot the eye in with black outliner. Outline the sea horse in silver and leave it to dry.

8. Remove the paper template from beneath the acrylic sheet and replace the masking tape. Paint the sea horse with diluted turquoise paint, taking care not to go over the outlines. Leave your work to dry.

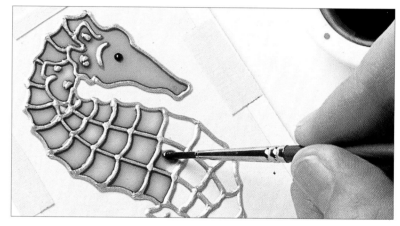

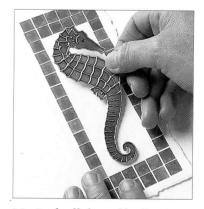

9. Cover the back of the sea horse with spray adhesive and mount on the piece of mirror card. Cut round the sea horse shape with scissors.

10. Place adhesive pads down the back of the sea horse, trimming them to fit the shape if necessary.

11. Peel off the self-adhesive backing and press the sea horse into place in the middle of the mosaic border.

The finished card
*A matching gift tag has been made
using squares of mosaic.*

Templates

gift tag

templates on this page shown full-size

Seasonal Greetings

This project introduces the use of white, which is the only opaque glass paint. A combination of techniques gives this card a really frosty feel. Glitter is sprinkled on the paint before it dries to add extra sparkle. Then the painted acetate is mounted on 3-D effect holographic card, which shimmers through the design. The snowman's hat and scarf may look tricky, but are fiddly rather than complicated. If you do not want to paint in such small areas, the scarf and hatband can be completed in one solid colour.

You will need

Acetate sheet 9 x 13cm
(3½ x 5¼ in)

Holographic card 9 x 13cm
(3½ x 5¼ in)

Blue mirror card 20 x 14cm
(8¼ x 5½ in)

Outliners: black and white

Glass paints: white, red, turquoise, orange, yellow, green, purple and clear

Glitter

Masking tape

Brush No.4

Palette

Newspaper

Full-size template

Gift tag template

1. Outline the design with black outliner. Let it dry completely, then paint in the body of the snowman with white paint, taking care not to paint over the outlines.

2. Protect the work surface with newspaper. While the white paint is still wet, sprinkle the head and body of the snowman with glitter. Leave your work to dry.

3. Brush off any loose glitter from the sections which have not yet been painted.

4. Paint the hat bobble white, then paint in all the red areas of the design.

5. Varying the colours to produce a pleasing effect, paint in the hatband and the scarf.

6. Fill in the background arch with diluted turquoise paint. Set your work aside to dry.

7. Cut out the snowman design and fix it to the holographic card with spray adhesive. Cut off the excess.

8. Score and fold the blue mirror card. Coat the back of the holographic card with spray adhesive and press it into place.

9. Add blobs of white outliner over the pale turquoise sky to represent snowflakes, and allow them to dry.

The finished card
*The pattern used for the scarf and hatband has
been repeated to produce a matching gift tag.*

Templates

Note

The card templates on this page have been reduced in size. To use, blow up on a photocopier set at 150 per cent.

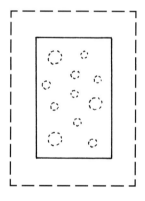

gift tags

Birthday wishes

The shops are brimming with birthday cards, but this is your chance to produce something a little different. This design is a bit fiddly to outline, so it is drawn on the acetate using a technical pen with water-based ink. The coloured areas of the design are filled in with solvent-based glass paints – as the lines are drawn with water-based pen, if you used water-based glass paint it would remove the pen line. Note that this card uses two folds. For an attractive matching gift tag, choose one of the motifs and make up a small window card.

You will need

Thick white card 9 x 18cm (3½ x 7in)

Acetate sheet 8 x 18cm (3¼ x 7in)

Gold card 24 x 18cm (9½ x 7in)

Tracing paper

Technical pen (0.5mm nib)

Water-based draughting film ink

Solvent-based glass paints: red, yellow and turquoise

Brush No.2

Gold outliner

Methylated spirit

Masking tape

Double-sided adhesive tape

Scissors

Pencil

Scalpel

Cutting mat

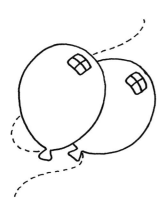

Full-size template

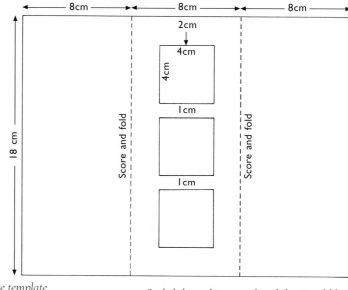

Scaled-down diagram of card showing folds

1. Referring to the diagram opposite, use a pencil and ruler to draw the two fold lines and the positions of the apertures on the gold card. Cut out the three apertures using a scalpel and a cutting mat. Score the fold lines.

2. Tape the clean acetate to a piece of thick white card, with the pattern in between. Outline the designs using a technical pen, avoiding the dotted lines, then leave your work to dry for ten minutes.

3. Paint in the coloured areas, making sure that you paint over the pen lines to seal the pen work. Leave your work to dry.

4. Using the gold outliner, decorate the present motif with dots. Outline the balloon strings and add the candle flames and cake filling. Leave to dry.

5. Remove the template and the card backing from the design. Lay the card face down on a flat surface. Position the acetate panel, also face down, so that the motifs lie centrally in each window. Secure with small pieces of masking tape.

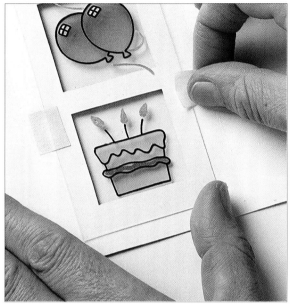

6. Place strips of double-sided tape around the acetate panel and peel off the backing. Do not worry if the card looks messy at this stage, as the flap will cover it.

7. Using a scalpel, trim a strip 2mm (1/16 in) wide off the edge of the card that will fold in to form the backing for the acetate panel.

8. Fold the left flap of the card base over on the middle section and press it flat, so that it adheres to the tape.

9. Using the dotted line on the paper as reference, draw the balloon strings on to the card with pencil. Go over the pencil lines with the gold outliner, then leave it to dry.

The finished card and gift tag

Templates

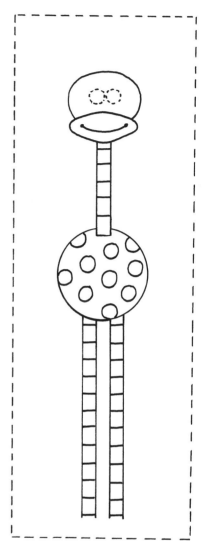

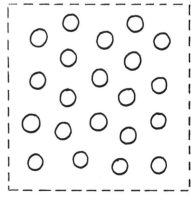

gift tag

templates on this page shown actual size

Valentine Heart

What better way to say 'I love you' than with a beautiful handmade card, and what better way to finish the book than with a messy project? The heart is created by daubing paint on pieces of acetate and pressing them together to make patterns. The pieces are pulled apart, left to dry, then cut into shapes and backed with mirror card. To finish, the heart is simply mounted on a pretty piece of card.

You will need

Acetate sheets 12 x 12cm
(4¾ x 4¾ in) x 2

Thick card

Silver mirror card 8 x 9cm
(3⅛x 3½ in)

Corrugated card 9 x 20cm
(3½ x 7¾ in)

Tracing paper

Thin card

Undiluted glass paints: pink
and purple

Water-based felt tip pen

Double-sided adhesive pads

Large brush

Spray adhesive

Scissors

*actual size templates
for card and gift tag*

1. Daub the squares of acetate generously with pink and purple paint.

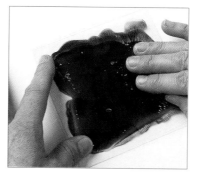

2. Press one square on the other, painted sides together. Apply pressure with your fingertips to merge the paint.

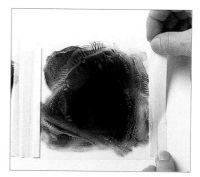

3. Pull the squares apart and tape them on to a piece of thick card to prevent them warping. Leave to dry.

4. Draw or trace a heart design, transfer it to thin card and cut it out.

5. Lay the heart shape on the un-painted side of one of the acetate squares. Draw round the shape with a water-based felt tip pen.

6. Cut out the heart shape. Coat the painted side with spray glue and press it on to a piece of mirror card. Cut round the heart shape again.

7. Score and fold the piece of corrugated card, score it down the middle, then fold it in half. Fix the heart to the card using double-sided adhesive pads.

The finished card

Templates

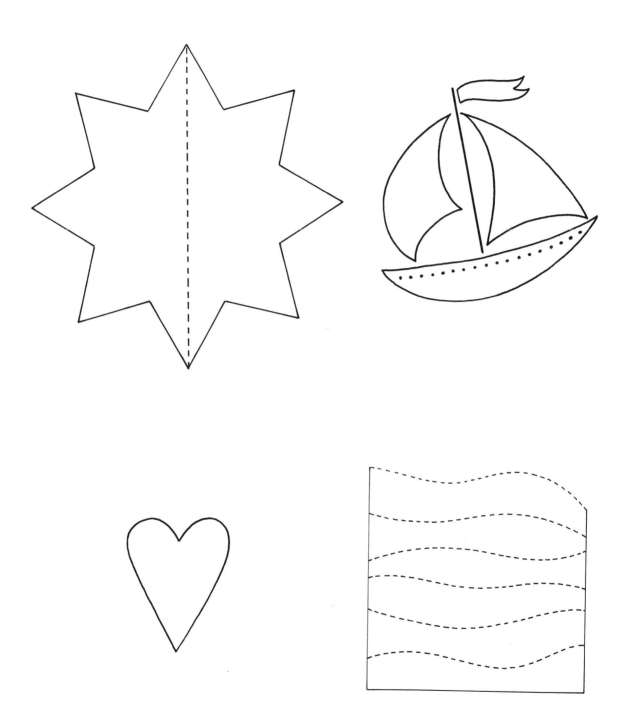

templates on this page shown actual size

Templates

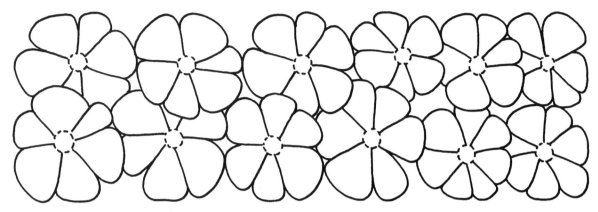

design from page 5

design from page 3

cover design

Index